purchasing

adding value to your business through effective supply management

editorial director:	Tom Nash
managing editor:	Lesley Shutte
sub-editor:	Caroline Proud
production manager:	Lisa Robertson
design:	Halo Design
commercial director:	Ed Hicks
managing director:	Andrew Main Wilson
chairman:	George Cox

Published for the IoD, The Chartered Institute of Purchasing
& Supply, PMMS Consulting Group and Xchanging
Procurement Services, by Director Publications Ltd,
116 Pall Mall, London SW1Y 5ED
T 020 7766 8910   W www.iod.com

The Chartered Institute of Purchasing & Supply (CIPS)

The Chartered Institute of Purchasing & Supply (CIPS) is the leading international body representing purchasing and supply management professionals.

It is the worldwide centre of excellence on purchasing and supply management issues. CIPS has over 33,000 members in 120 different countries, including senior business people, high ranking civil servants and leading academics.

The activities of purchasing and supply management professionals can have a major impact on the profitability and efficiency of all types of organisation. Purchasing and supply management professionals also control huge budgets and, in the UK alone, collectively spend over £1,100bn a year.

PMMS Consulting Group

PMMS Consulting Group is the leading purchasing and supply chain consultancy with 25 years' experience at the buyer-seller interface.

With two UK and seven international offices combined with a network of consultants worldwide, PMMS operates across the globe in both the public and private sectors for over 30 of the world's top companies. The group has specialist divisions for consultancy, negotiation, skills development, recruitment and e-procurement, and offers outstanding expertise with a truly global perspective.

Our clear mission is to bring tangible improvements to the business performance of our clients, by the implementation of innovative and effective concepts and processes.

Xchanging Procurement Services

Xchanging Procurement Services delivers best-in-class integrated procurement services to leading corporations and an opportunity for partner-suppliers to operate more efficiently. Through Xchanging's unique focus on procurement processes, service levels and price, procurement is turned from an overhead to a revenue generator.

Xchanging offers a new model for procurement outsourcing that enables companies to achieve world-class procurement capability rapidly, in non-core and, in some cases, core categories of spend.

Xchanging Procurement Services is currently managing over £200m of spend for its clients, who include BAE SYSTEMS, Novar and Heywood Williams.

CONTENTS

Xchanging

Unparalleled
Category Expertise

Radical Improvement of Non-core Activities

For further Information
please contact
Mary Norris
Xchanging Procurement Services

Telephone: 07831 411728
email: mnorris@xchanging.com

www.xchanging.com

buying into success

George Cox, Director General
Institute of Directors

World-class companies have no doubt about the importance of purchasing and supply management in today's highly competitive world.

Whether you call it supply chain management, purchasing, procurement, or any combination of these terms, the fact is that this is a vital management issue which delivers substantial rewards to those organisations that get it right. The most obvious benefit is a direct improvement to the bottom line from cost-saving. But there are other significant benefits, such as enhanced reputation, quality, reliability, product innovation and differentiation, and speed to market.

However, while some companies acknowledge the importance of the area, many fail to address the issues as thoroughly and systematically as they might, often failing to take advantage of recent best practice.

This Director's Guide will help directors appraise their current purchasing and supply management policies. It poses key questions, such as how to ascertain the level of expertise held by in-house staff, whether to develop or outsource, and how to adopt appropriate supplier/purchaser relationships that best suit a particular company's objectives – whether they be collaborative, adversarial or mixed.

It also offers practical advice on how to make improvements, such as how best to utilise e-sourcing and e-procurement to enhance overall purchasing and supply management effectiveness.

why purchasing is key

Purchasing and supply management is of critical strategic importance. Roy Ayliffe, director of professional practice of The Chartered Institute of Purchasing & Supply, explains why

Without effective strategies to co-ordinate purchasing and to manage supply lines, organisations lose their way: costs spiral out of control; customers and members of the public are let down and the reputation of the organisation is damaged. Purchasing and supply management, therefore, should not be seen as a backroom, peripheral function but as a key business process.

In today's high-pressure environment, the role of purchasing and supply management has additional importance. For organisations of all types, the challenge is to improve the quality of products and services while driving down costs. This chapter explains how good purchasing and supply management practices can help to square that circle.

cutting costs, improving efficiency

EXECUTIVE SUMMARY

- ☐ organisations spend 30-80 per cent of turnover with suppliers
- ☐ improvements in purchasing and supply management will have a direct impact on the bottom line and on service and on reputation
- ☐ only a co-ordinated, boardroom-led approach will deliver optimum benefits
- ☐ Purchasing and supply management must be an integral part of organisational strategy

Over the past few decades, efforts to cut costs have tended to focus on head-count. The elimination of unnecessary activities, productivity drives, automation and contracting out (or outsourcing) have all seen workforces shrink. Although right and necessary in many cases, such programmes have obvious drawbacks.

They increase short-term costs, are time consuming to administer and, if not properly managed, run the risk of creating severe staff morale problems – possibly leading to industrial action. They can also store up trouble for the future: if you let good staff go you might have a skills crisis when things pick up again.

The emphasis on personnel reduction has been combined with action to reduce the number of facilities required to run the business. This has resulted in the amalgamation or shut down of manufacturing plants and sales, service and administration offices.

In lots of organisations, such 're-engineering' is now complete. Having exhausted opportunities to save money by cutting staff numbers and rationalising operations, directors are having to look elsewhere.

Procurement is the obvious place. This is because the value of bought-in goods and services is usually a high percentage of turnover or revenue. The amount varies from 30 to 80 per cent. The figures per sector are as follows:

- general goods manufacturing and retail – 65 per cent to 70 per cent
- electronics and aviation – up to 80 per cent
- the process sector (pharmaceuticals, oil and food industries) – 30 per cent to 40 per cent
- the service sector (banking and insurance) – 30 per cent to 40 per cent

---

CASE STUDY: BRITISH AIRWAYS

It has been a difficult few years for the world's major airlines. Even before two hijacked planes flew into the twin towers of New York's World Trade Center on 11 September 2001, economic downturn was hitting them hard as demand for business travel fell away

Since that fateful day, things have gone from bad to worse as a result of the deteriorating business climate, the threat of further terrorist attacks, the war on Iraq and panic over the SARS virus.

In February 2002, British Airways responded to this crisis with a new business plan entitled "Future Size and Shape". The plan called for 13,000 job losses and annualised cost savings of £650m a year by March 2004. In February this year, it stepped up the pressure to reduce costs by setting a target of an additional £450m in savings.

CASE STUDY: BRITISH AIRWAYS

This has put the airline's procurement function firmly in the hot seat. At the company's annual investor day earlier this year, BA's procurement director, Silla Maizey, was asked to address major shareholders and financial analysts for the first time, explaining how the airline will shave £300m, or 10 per cent, off its annual purchasing bill by 2005. Good progress has already been made, she says, with £95m of procurement and IT savings signed off by the end of March 2003.

These savings have been achieved partly by negotiating lower prices through electronic auctions (which has saved over £20m) and by channelling a greater proportion of spend through fewer suppliers. BA has already cut its supply base from 14,000 to 5,000 and aims to further reduce it to just 2,000.

But costs are also now being taken out by managing the internal demand for goods and services more effectively, and by reining in specifications so that money is not wasted on unnecessary features. This has meant creating a different mindset among the 200 members of the procurement department and following a more rigorous and consistent approach to purchasing.

"Historically through price, we were able to deliver two to three per cent reductions in the external cost base," notes Maizey's boss, BA's chief financial officer, John Rishton. "Through deeper implementation of the strategic sourcing process, we are able to consider savings of 10 per cent."

Procurement, Rishton concludes, is now "recognised as essential to our business, not just an 'add on' support department".

Geraint John

In both the process and the service sectors, the values will equal, if not exceed, the amount spent on payroll and facilities.

In the public sector, expenditure on goods and services is in the region of 50 per cent of total expenditure.

It is clear, then, that cutting the cost of in-bought goods, services and capital items can make a dramatic improvement to an organisation's bottom line. The pie chart on page 10 shows cost of supplies, other costs and profit as percentages of turnover in an average company.

A simple calculation shows that if the company in our example saved just 10 per cent of its total spend on purchases, its profit would increase by five per cent of turnover, nearly doubling to 11 per cent.

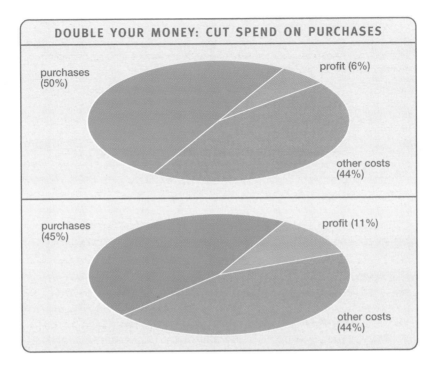

DOUBLE YOUR MONEY: CUT SPEND ON PURCHASES

purchases (50%)

profit (6%)

other costs (44%)

purchases (45%)

profit (11%)

other costs (44%)

creating value, improving effectiveness

Raising the standard of purchasing and supply management can create benefits far beyond price reductions for goods and services. In many instances, it is the ability to get suppliers and the supply chain to perform in ways that serve the purchasing organisation better that provides the real benefits.

Few things illustrate this more than building and refurbishment contracts. Suppose, for example, you are a retailer, about to refurbish your sites. You want the work to be done well to guarantee the maximum long-term return on your investment, but you want your outlets to be able to re-open as soon as possible. By carefully evaluating the supply market, by inviting the right companies to tender for your business and by working together with the selected contractor, you can get the value for money you need and keep the number of lost trading days down to a minimum. Conversely, if you fail to manage the procurement process in this way the project is likely to drift on, incurring more costs and losing you more money.

CASE STUDY: PLYMOUTH HOSPITALS NHS TRUST

NHS hospitals are under intense pressure to treat more patients, more quickly, and to make more effective use of taxpayers' money

The service provided by the the cardiothoracic department at Plymouth Hospitals NHS Trust, which serves 430,000 people in west Devon and east Cornwall, has been significantly improved by an innovative approach to purchasing key products.

Heart disease is the UK's biggest killer, and demand for treatment is growing by more than 30 per cent a year. Waiting lists are long; budgets are severely stretched.

Despite this, the department had, until the new initiative began in 1998, failed to take a strategic approach to procurement. "Purchasing activity was highly fragmented, buying decisions were made ad hoc by clinical staff, and there was little or no negotiation with suppliers," explains Ian Shepherd, the trust's director of purchasing and supply.

Twelve hundred products were being purchased from 35 different manufacturers.

Instead of following the old route of awarding contracts product by product, the team of clinicians and purchasing experts decided to put out one invitation to tender for all the department's core requirements, including pacemakers, heart valves and diagnostic devices, representing around 80 per cent of its £9m annual expenditure.

The results have been impressive. Cost savings of £1.7m, or 19 per cent, have been made against a target of 10-15 per cent. The average cost of treating a patient has fallen from £496 to £258, enabling an extra 450 people to be treated.

There is far more cohesion in purchasing activity. The department now purchases 560 products from just three primary suppliers. The burden on administrative staff is lower; the clinical risk for doctors and nurses using the equipment is reduced.

Shepherd has now expanded his purchasing team and is beginning to introduce similar philosophies to other departments, not only at the Plymouth Trust but throughout Devon and Cornwall. Within the next five years, he hopes to achieve additional savings of £15m. "We are challenging the status quo in the health service, thinking differently about how goods and services are purchased," he says.

Looking further ahead, the purchasing department is talking to equipment suppliers about the potential of robotics and other automated technologies to improve the next generation of NHS hospitals – whether it be assisting with surgery or simply moving products around.

Geraint John

Good relationships with suppliers also enable existing products to be improved or enhanced and new products or services to be brought to market quickly and efficiently. In some cases, suppliers can be brought into the product-design process. A kind of technology transfer can take place, whereby purchasers and suppliers swap skills in order to achieve product innovation. The international audio equipment manufacturer Bose, for example, has used supplier-in-plant personnel as authorised links between its design teams and its suppliers. This has allowed it to free members of staff for other purchasing duties such as communications and material cost reductions.

If your suppliers are your partners, you can introduce joint cost-cutting initiatives. The DIY retailer, B&Q, for example, has made a point of trying to eliminate packaging waste in its supply chain. This not only saves everyone money – packaging and transportation costs both fall – but also helps the company fulfil its pledge to the consumer to be environmentally aware.

the purchasing and supply management challenge

The purchasing and supply management process will only deliver optimum benefits if it is a coherent whole, if the disparate and often dispersed people involved in purchasing decisions work together for the good of the organisation.

You cannot simply bolt-on a discrete purchasing and supply management function and hope for the best. Nor can you assume that the diverse groups involved in the procurement process will come together naturally to work things out – experience shows that each function pursues its own interests to the exclusion of others.

BENEFITS OF EFFECTIVE PURCHASING AND SUPPLY MANAGEMENT

- [ ] lower costs and better value for money
- [ ] security of supply – certainty that vital raw materials and components will continue to flow to the organisation
- [ ] better risk control – sourcing policies that do not damage the company's reputation, conflict with social and environmental responsibilities or contravene legislation
- [ ] leverage – the ability to negotiate better deals from suppliers
- [ ] quality improvements – supplier relationships that make products and services better and reduce time to market
- [ ] process efficiency – the use of electronic and technological tools to improve ordering and related processes

THE KEY PURCHASING AND SUPPLY MANAGEMENT TASKS

The role of the director responsible for purchasing and supply is to:

- [ ] ensure the purchasing and supply management perspective directly relates to business needs

- [ ] select and implement the appropriate strategies to support the organisation's goals

- [ ] advise on, and help to implement, strategic changes such as mergers and acquisitions, making sure synergies are exploited and the maximum commercial leverage obtained

- [ ] arrange appropriate outsourcing of corporate services – with the objective of delivering significant quality improvements and reductions in costs

- [ ] set continuous targets for improvement, providing training for colleagues and those with significant purchasing responsibilities

- [ ] use a range of tools, methodologies and approaches that can add significant value to the organisation with year-on-year improvements

- [ ] keep up with developments in purchasing and supply management through networking

- [ ] keep abreast of new techniques

A co-ordinated, boardroom-led approach is needed – otherwise supply failures and excessive costs are likely to result.

Purchasing and supply management decisions must be consistent with the organisation's objectives and culture and ethos and be compatible with its structure and geographical reach. The board should resist jumping on the bandwagon of purchasing fads and fashions and rather ask: does this suit us?

There are many types of purchasing and supply management strategies. Good purchasing and supply management people use the right ones, at the right times. (See box: The key purchasing and supply management tasks.) And they usually discharge their responsibilities best by working within cross-functional teams.

getting started

Re-orienting purchasing and supply management in your organisation is not easy. It takes time and demands commitment and might require investment in training and technology.

The starting point is a review, an audit of current procedures. (See box: Six questions that the CEO should ask.) Once the review is complete, you can decide on the action that needs to be taken and start to move forward. (Chapter 3 explains how.)

conclusion

Effective purchasing and supply management helps organisations to win – and sustain – competitive advantage. Provided it is, from the outset, backed by the very top, upgrading the purchasing and supply management process can be one of the best investments an organisation ever makes.

SIX QUESTIONS THAT THE CEO SHOULD ASK

How do you re-position purchasing and supply management to deliver competitive edge? CEOs and other senior directors and managers should begin by finding the answers to the following questions:

1. how much of our turnover is spent on bought-in goods and services? How does the percentage compare with that spent on manpower and facilities?

2. who is purchasing the key goods, services and capital items within our organisation? Do they have sufficient knowledge and understanding of how the supply market works? (Don't confuse this with product knowledge.)

3. is our purchasing and supply management operation governed by a set of bureaucratic regulations or can our people operate in the market in a manner that meets the needs of the business? Are they trained to do so?

4. do we have a purchasing and supply management department in our organisation? Do they purchase the pencils or the plant? Would we trust them to purchase the more important purchases?

5. are we confident that we will be able to purchase key goods and services economically in the future? If so, why?

6. do we purchase everything in the same way? Do we have different methodologies for high- and low-value and high- and low-risk purchases?

view from the board

What are purchasing's key imperatives? Geraint John, editor of Supply Management magazine, asks leading chief executives for their views

That purchasing and supply management is business-critical is increasingly being acknowledged by the world's leading chief executives. At last year's conference of The Chartered Institute of Purchasing and Supply, Sir Nick Scheele, president and chief operating officer of Ford Motor Company, was unequivocal. "Purchasing," he said, "controls the ultimate profitability of the company."

But what exactly do boards want from their purchasing or procurement departments? The answer is a combination of operational efficiency and strategic effectiveness.

EXECUTIVE SUMMARY

- the primary operational role is to guarantee security of supply
- value for money is more important than rock-bottom price
- the management of internal and external relationships must be consistent with strategy and ethos
- the primary strategic roles are to drive out innovation and stimulate growth

security of supply

Getting in the goods and services to keep the business running is still priority number one. "We have to be sure that our service and manufacturing operations are adequately supplied with everything they require," says Alan Wood, chief executive of Siemens in the UK. And he expects them to be supplied "as smoothly and as efficiently as possible".

For private healthcare provider BUPA, security of supply means always having the right instruments in an operating theatre, or the right ingredients for its patients' meals. To its chief executive, Val Gooding, not being able to provide what the customer is paying for is simply unthinkable. Gooding wants to be certain that suppliers chosen by her purchasing team are not going to let the company down – that "risk in the supply chain is managed".

But the ability to source adequate supplies from reliable companies in the timeframe required is only one definition of good purchasing. The purchasing and supply management function also has to ensure that, in Gooding's words, "everything is available at the right price and at the right quality".

value for money

One of the most common complaints levelled against purchasing departments is that they care too much about cost and too little about quality.

Cost reduction is certainly high on many board agendas, particularly in today's tougher business environment. And because every pound saved on external spend is potentially a pound added to the bottom line, boards see purchasing as central to cost control.

However, purchase price is only one variable in the cost equation. As Peter Gershon, chief executive of the Office of Government Commerce (OGC), the procurement advisory body for central government, and a former director of British Aerospace, says: "If procurement is seen as focusing basically on price, then it is tactical, low-value-added and likely to be of little or no interest to the board.

"Procurement decisions should be based on value for money, which is defined as the optimal combination of whole-life costs and quality to meet users' business requirements".

In the case of a new office building, taking a whole-life cost (or 'total cost of ownership') approach means not only looking at the cost of designing and constructing the premises in the first place, but also the subsequent cost of things such as heating and maintenance.

"The likelihood," says Gershon, "is that the building with the lowest initial cost is not the one that will give me the lowest lifecycle cost."

management of relationships

Keen as chief executives are to pay less for bought-in goods and services, they also care about business relationships. Internally, they want to ensure that, where appropriate, purchasing is pooling common requirements across the company, or between different divisions, in order to get the best volume deals from suppliers. But, at the same time, they don't want the flexibility of business units to be restricted.

Externally, they want to ensure they are perceived as professional and fair and to be seen to be treating their suppliers as they would like to be treated themselves. "As a chief executive," explains Gooding, "you don't want your suppliers to feel that they are going to be subject to an overbearing, bullying style of procurement, or something that is driven absolutely by rock-bottom price."

"There is a danger that you can drive your suppliers too hard," agrees Alan Wood. "That may be OK for a year or two, but sooner or later if they get into trouble, you're in trouble as well." In any case, Wood adds, you can't always achieve cost savings in isolation; sometimes you need to work in partnership with suppliers, helping them to reduce their own costs – as opposed to just trying to cut their profit margins – in the expectation that the savings will be passed on to you in the form of lower prices.

innovation and value

Working with suppliers to take cost out of a supply chain is only one element of the partnership approach. Innovation, in the sense of developing new products and services, and doing it quicker or better than competitors, is what differentiates successful companies from the rest. Gooding believes purchasing is often 'the unsung hero' when it comes to innovation. "That's probably quite right – you don't want to keep banging on to your customers about your purchasing department. But some of the big steps forward in industry are delivered by purchasing people when you dig right down."

These days, much of that innovation is likely to come from your supply base. In the automotive industry, for example, the big car makers now depend on suppliers to deliver entire assemblies rather than individual components. "We don't manufacture very much," says Ford's Scheele. "We manufacture engines, we manufacture stamps and body panels, we put them together and then we trim out the car. But everything else is purchased. So suppliers are critical; they in large measure determine the technological level we have, the quality level, and really how the vehicle feels and drives."

Managing those strategic relationships and ensuring that suppliers are handled with respect and in an ethical manner is essential if Ford is to become "the customer of choice", Scheele adds. This, combined with the fact that cars are full of rapidly evolving computer technology, means that "purchasing can now add far, far more value than it could in the past".

Value is also what the customer is looking for when they purchase a car. That isn't something that is defined by the manufacturer, argues Scheele; it is something the customer decides is worth paying for. Weighing up what features to include versus the cost involved is obviously a key issue for marketing and product-development teams, but purchasing also has an important role, he says. "Purchasing is a major player in making sure that value as ascribed by a customer is value as we buy it from a supplier."

profitability and growth

Simon Beech, managing director of Bulwell Precision Engineers, a 240-employee firm based in Pinxton, Nottinghamshire, confirms the importance of purchasing's strategic role. As a supplier of aero engines and airframes, Bulwell has found that big customers such as Rolls-Royce and Airbus are very interested in how it manages its own supply chain. "Manufacturing is a given now," Beech says. "Customers assume you do that well. What's crucial is the value of the service you can provide them. That partly depends on our supply base, and so we see purchasing and supply chain management as a selling point. It's key to our future growth."

That perspective is shared by Richard Cumber, managing director of Feedwater, a specialist water treatment company that employs 50 staff in the Wirral. "Purchasing should be as effective in promoting business growth as it is in controlling costs," he says. "By working cleverly with our suppliers through strategic alliances – by sharing information, for example, or getting goods on a just-in-time basis – we can deliver better value for money to our clients and enhance our profitability."

Another business leader who believes strongly that purchasing can influence growth is Tony Isaac, chief executive of industrial gases producer the BOC Group. The company even calls its purchasing function "supply management" to reflect its broader role. "I expect supply management to help the entire organisation create competitive advantage," he says. It can do this in many ways, from identifying and developing sources of supply in emerging markets, through to advising on mergers and acquisitions and facilitating new product design.

strategic alignment

Like other chief executives, Isaac expects his purchasing team to use best-practice processes and procedures, but always to be looking for new and better ways of doing things. It needs to have a clear understanding of the business strategy and to work closely with other parts of the company in achieving their objectives, he says.

On both these fronts, purchasing departments have plenty of room for improvement, reckons the OGC's Gershon. They also need to be able to "speak the language of top management, not talk in jargon". But while purchasing professionals must be capable of rising to the challenge, "it is for boards, whether in the public or private sector, to decide what they want of the procurement process. Is it tactical or is it strategic?"

Gershon's own view is clear. Procurement, he concludes, "is an important, proven source of value added if looked at in a strategic context. So why would anyone deny themselves the opportunity of taking advantage of it?"

upgrading the procurement process

Brian Court, director and senior consultant with PMMS Consulting Group, offers a step-by-step guide to re-orienting purchasing's role

How does an organisation go about upgrading its purchasing process? The purpose of this chapter is to provide a general 'road map'.

identifying the spend pattern

As chapter 1 made clear, the first step is to identify the extent and nature of current expenditure on bought-in goods, services and capital items. It is important to note that these data should include all corporate expenditure – regardless of who is actually doing the purchasing.

A review of the purchase ledger will provide information on all requisitions. These should then be arranged in ascending order of value. Starting with the lowest-value order, it will be possible to plot a graph that tracks the cumulative number of orders against their cumulative value. In most organisations that have been studied, the graph will be similar to the one on the next page.

The cumulative value of the 50 per cent lowest-value orders (Category A) will amount to less than two per cent of the total value of the spend. At the other end of the scale, the highest-value 20 per cent (Category B) will account for 80 per cent of total spend.

EXECUTIVE SUMMARY

- ☐ cost reduction efforts should focus on high-value items
- ☐ reviews of purchasing must reflect the external factors influencing the organisation
- ☐ moves to strategic purchasing inevitably demand new skills
- ☐ purchasers must be capable of creating value in the supply chain and of adapting to changing business needs

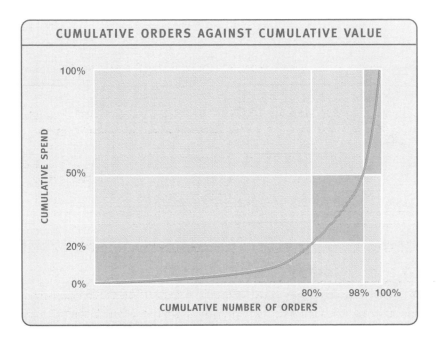

CUMULATIVE ORDERS AGAINST CUMULATIVE VALUE

resource usage

The next step is to look at the resources dedicated to the purchase of these two categories. In most organisations, too much time is spent on Category A items and too little time on Category B items.

There is usually no economic case for strenuous efforts to drive down Category A prices. The cost of processing the order and paying the bill (circa £35-£80) may far exceed the cost of the item itself. Even if you could reduce the cost of Category A items by 20 per cent, you would still only reduce the goods and services bill by 0.4 per cent of total spend. Clearly, unless the items are of a critical nature, the effort cannot be justified.

Category B items are high-cost. Here, cost savings and quality improvements really count. Category B purchases need to be managed with great care; the organisation needs to ensure that those involved in purchasing them have the skill to get the best out of the market. All too often, key orders are placed by personnel who, while being highly expert in their field, have no idea about how supply markets work and how to extract the greatest benefit from suppliers.

> **PURCHASING HORRORS**
>
> ☐ a major finance house placed a contract for a £20m IT development project on the strength of one sheet of paper, leaving little remedy for non-performance and creating high exposure to cost increases
>
> ☐ a manufacturer of a basic building material ordered a locomotive to shunt railcars throughout the site, only to find that it had insufficient power, and there was no contractual remedy
>
> ☐ a high security printing organisation spent millions on purchasing special paper from one supplier over 20 years with price based on a formula. Market research showed that the price paid was three times the market norm

The naivety of these personnel can be breathtaking – see the 'purchasing horrors' panel above, for some real-life examples.

In many instances it will be necessary to get the supply market to change to meet the business needs of the purchasing organisation. This demands specialist skill.

re-orientation

When the analysis of expenditure and use of human resources has been completed, it will be possible for senior management to decide whether there is a case for upgrading the purchasing process. If there is, there is usually only one option: a fundamental re-orientation of procurement and its associated operations.

The change will involve four major organisational elements:

☐ role (mission and identity)

☐ relationships

☐ systems and organisation

☐ resources

These elements are represented on the diagram on page 24, which is based on the work of PMMS consultant, J N Parkin. The diagram puts individuals at the centre of the organisation, surrounded by the four key elements. Outside the organisation is the multi-layered environment that is so influential. Working outwards, the layers include the trading environment, the image environment and the macro (political and economic) environment.

When making a change, organisations should ideally start from outside the wheel, looking at external influences and what impact they have or will have on role. They should then move clockwise through relationships, systems, and finally resources.

This sequence is contrary to the way people learn about the organisation in which they are involved. In nearly all cases, understanding of the job moves anti-clockwise around the Parkin wheel. So the individual first learns about resources (office, transport, computers, secretarial staff). Then comes an understanding of systems (how to set up a meeting, book travel and accommodation). After a longer period of time, the individual begins to build a network of relationships with customers, suppliers, bosses, peers and subordinates. Next comes more clarity about mission or identity as the individual begins to set his or her role in context. Finally, the impact of the environment becomes increasingly apparent.

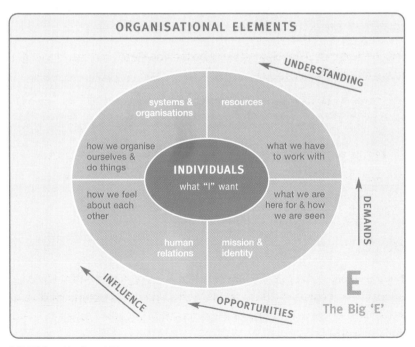

© PMMS Consulting Group 2002

24

Following the Parkin model may seem counter-intuitive. But it will avoid costly mistakes. The box 'A warehouse too far' on page 26 illustrates why.

change considerations

environment

At the macro level, companies will need to understand the economic influences, for example:

- ☐ are interest rates high or low and what is the outlook?
- ☐ is our market expanding or shrinking?
- ☐ are goods and services being drawn from politically unstable locations?

At the next level is the image environment. Senior management will need to evaluate the importance of the image of the company and decide on the extent to which image should determine sourcing policies. Do you want, as far as possible, to buy British? Do you want to cut companies that use child labour – or otherwise flout ethical codes – out of your supply chain?

The final and most direct influence will be the trading environment. Here, the management will need to answer questions such as:

- ☐ are our customers becoming more demanding?
- ☐ are their needs changing and, if so, what does it mean for us?
- ☐ do our suppliers give us priority or are we at the back of the queue?
- ☐ are our costs going up; can we recover them from customers?
- ☐ are we cash-rich or heavily geared?

role

In nearly all cases, change will mean visualising the organisation's purchasing process as a profit contributor rather than as a set of costly bureaucratic procedures. Time must be taken to ensure senior management acceptance and promotion of the new role.

A WAREHOUSE TOO FAR

A growing distribution company was experiencing increasing strains on warehouse capacity. The proposed solution was to build a large extension, which in turn would require additional manpower. Fortunately, the organisation pulled back from this costly initiative and decided to follow the Parkin model

The first review was of the role – what was the warehouse there for? It was concluded that the warehouse was part of the supply chain and that the objective of the supply chain was to be able to get goods to customers within a reasonable period of time.

Next came relationships with both customers and suppliers. Customers indicated that delivery within five days of order would be acceptable provided that the distribution company made every effort if an emergency situation arose. Suppliers agreed to offer an emergency three-day service as long as the distribution company minimised such requests.

Systems followed. The company installed a computer system that dramatically cut down the times required to process both customer demands and orders to suppliers.

The last consideration was resources. It was concluded that, with the introduction of these changes, stock holdings could be reduced. This meant that there was sufficient capacity in the existing warehouse and no extension or additional manpower was required.

If the company had used the incorrect sequence, it would have ended up with a larger warehouse that it really didn't need.

Having considered all of the external influences, the board must decide whether it is serious about wanting to re-orientate the procurement process. It must then state the intended goals of the change management programme. Examples of these goals are:

1. to manage the order placement process as efficiently as possible

2. to obtain goods and services of the right quality, at the right place and the right time

3. to meet the requirements of the budget holders, making cost reductions wherever possible

4. to provide a competitive edge in the purchase of goods and services

5. to manage the supply base so as to maximise overall performance and competitiveness

These goals are in ascending order of strategic importance. The first sees the process as a clerical function with the emphasis on efficiency. The second is service-orientated, designed to provide users with what they want (as opposed to what they need). Neither of these has the capacity to make dramatic improvements to corporate performance.

Number 3 identifies a specific, but somewhat limited, role of cost reduction based on specifications previously determined by others. It will be essentially reactive and severely limit the ability to make strategic improvements.

Number 4 presumes early involvement in the definition of requirements (specifications), thus facilitating a wider approach to the supply market. The last is the widest view of all, taking the line that the job is to manage the supply base and thus create the most favourable conditions for the purchasing organisation.

Having decided what it wants the purchasing process to achieve, the senior management team must promulgate the message throughout the entire organisation. It must also be prepared to overcome objections and opposition – whether derived from genuine concerns or from entrenched positions. If it cannot justify its proposals it should think again.

relationships

Once the role of the purchasing process is agreed there needs to be redefinition of the relationships between all the parties that influence it. As chapter 1 said, many parties have a role to play. The views and the requirements of all of them must be heard, but the interests of none of them should come before the interests of the organisation. An engineer, for example, might want a high-level specification whereas something of lower quality might be perfectly adequate.

The new structure must encourage all parties to work together with mutual respect and understanding, always with the overall corporate goals kept in focus. Commercial personnel must gain a better understanding of technical issues. Those with technical skills must be helped to gain a better understanding of commercial realities.

systems

In turn, this will lead to the development of a new set of policies and practices that creates the framework for effective management and development of the

CASE STUDY: BRITISH SKY BROADCASTING

When new and fast-growing companies are focused on establishing their business and on increasing their market share, the way employees buy in goods and services tends to be a fairly low priority. But over time, the desire for a tighter rein on costs – and hence a more professional approach to procurement – invariably moves up the board's agenda

A good example is the FTSE 100 television company British Sky Broadcasting (BSkyB). Since entering the UK market in 1989, Sky has grown rapidly through aggressive acquisition of sports and movie rights, major investment in a digital platform and heavy marketing. It now boasts almost seven million subscribers and generates more than £3bn in annual revenues.

In 2000, the senior management team didn't know exactly how much the company was spending with external suppliers – only that it was a significant amount. It vowed to get better value for money.

Tim Ussher, who joined Sky as its first director of procurement in May 2001, puts the spend figure at around £1bn, excluding broadcast rights. Working closely with managers throughout the company, he and his 18-strong team were able to save £85m within the first 18 months. They conducted thorough reviews of each supply market, sought bids from a wider sample of suppliers, and negotiated better deals.

The two biggest areas of spend, accounting for more than £300m annually, are the set-top boxes and satellite dishes given to subscribers to enable them to receive Sky's channels, and marketing. These directly affect one of Sky's key financial metrics, subscriber acquisition cost (SAC) – in other words, how much it costs to sign up a new customer, then supply and install the equipment in their home.

Between September 2001 and March 2003, the SAC fell from around £250 per customer to £210, thanks largely to the achievement of a 35 per cent reduction in the price paid for boxes and dishes.

Procurement's influence now extends across more than 80 categories of goods and services, including telecommunications, IT and broadcasting equipment. It has also been supporting the company's corporate social responsibility project, and has even been asked to review its pensions provision and insurance needs.

"Whether it's for stationery or satellite transponders, everyone at Sky now understands the value of a professional, transparent procurement process," says Ussher. "That's a big step forward for this company."

Geraint John

supply market. Here, the most important step must be to develop purchasing procedures and practices that can facilitate a more entrepreneurial approach. Rigid rules, such as demanding that three competitive bids be obtained in all circumstances, should be avoided. Highly trained staff should be empowered with the flexibility to purchase in the most effective manner, consistent with market circumstances – subject, of course, to proper audit scrutiny.

As the organisation develops, management will need to decide on the levels of IT support that are to be provided. These can vary from very simple automated record keeping through to full-blown electronic procurement systems.

resources

With role, relationships and systems further clarified, it will then be possible to decide on staff quality and resource level. Clearly, strategic purchasing requires a higher calibre of staff than 'back-office', 'clerical' purchasing. Most organisations that undertake an upgrade of the purchasing process find it necessary to make changes to at least some of their purchasing staff. The remainder nearly always require a substantial amount of re-education.

moving to strategic purchasing

Strategic purchasing can be defined as: "The development of ways of approaching and interacting with the supply market with the aim of maximising the contribution to corporate performance and profit now and in the future."

It assumes that purchasers can determine and change the supply market within which they function. This might involve any or all of the following:

- persuading a reluctant supplier to trade

- upgrading existing supplier performance

- creating a supply capability where none currently exists

- circumventing and outmanoeuvring cartels

- working with monopolies

There is no point in taking action that might give a short-term gain (eg. reducing the number of suppliers) if it results in a disadvantageous situation in the future (eg. monopoly supplier). The whole purpose of strategic purchasing is to enhance corporate performance. In turn, this means that any purchasing action must be closely aligned to business needs and objectives.

A world-class purchasing organisation is characterised by:

- [ ] segmentation of purchase portfolio

- [ ] development of long-term procurement strategies for key bought-in goods, services and capital items

- [ ] ongoing assessment of supply markets and suppliers

- [ ] evaluation of supplier attitudes and motivations

- [ ] regular assessment of the risks in the supply chain

- [ ] creative action to change the supply market to advantage

- [ ] promotion of the purchasing organisation as a preferred customer

Strategic purchasing will demand that commercial considerations are evaluated at every stage of a purchase – including concept and design. It will influence specifications and requirements, contributing up-to-date and in-depth knowledge of the market and the market place. And it will be persuasive in pointing out the commercial implications of pursuing a particular route, such as mergers, or technology.

technologies that optimise value

Mike Fogg, consultant specialising in e-procurement at PMMS Consulting Group, looks at the opportunities that e-procurement and e-sourcing present

E-procurement and e-sourcing can help to win competitive advantage.

E-sourcing can be defined as the use of the internet to inform purchasing decisions and strategies; e-procurement as the use of technologies to improve transactional processes.

The results can include:

- reduced unit prices for goods and services
- reduced process costs
- contraction of the clerical workforce
- shorter lead times
- lower risks
- technical innovations
- improved customer services
- lower inventory levels
- improved information flow

EXECUTIVE SUMMARY

- electronic ordering and payment systems cut processing costs and shorten delivery times
- the internet can help to identify alternative supply sources and increase bargaining power
- systems integration can improve stock control and accelerate new-product development
- online databases and order-tracking can improve customer services

The optimum benefits will, however, only be achieved if the relevant electronic tools are strategically deployed. The aim of this chapter is to promote the use of 'e-solutions' throughout the supply base while giving a realistic picture of their potential.

reducing unit prices

High-volume orders of standard items can amount to a six or seven figure spend. Get the unit cost of these down, therefore, and you will save a lot of money.

There are several ways in which information and communications technology (ICT) is helping to secure better deals.

The World Wide Web is strengthening negotiating positions by providing buyers and their researchers with more information on suppliers and their supply chain. Knowledge is power; it can win you leverage. One UK organisation found that a supplier had 'posted' the expected value of the sale it was going to make on the New York Stock Exchange. By using this information in negotiations, the company was able to make a substantial saving.

Unit price reductions are also flowing from e-tendering and from the aggregation of low-risk, low-cost items into electronic catalogues (see reducing process costs, opposite).

Perhaps the greatest potential for price cuts, however, lies in electronic reverse auctions. These are said to have achieved savings of up to 70 per cent on suppliers' previous 'best' offers. During the e-auction event, suppliers located at their own bases use standard PCs to place competitive bids for your business over a one or two-hour period. The deal is done 'live'; no hanging around for quotes.

There are caveats, however. The auction process demands more resources than you might think. You will need the help of an e-auction service provider – and you will need to make sure that the sale is well-managed and ethically run. As it takes place, you will have to be crystal clear about your specifications and requirements and you will have to communicate constantly with suppliers.

Moreover, e-auctions might not be suitable for every kind of deal. They can be perceived as confrontational tools by suppliers and have the potential, therefore, to sour good working relationships. Although good management can minimise the risks, it might be prudent to use e-auctions for price improvements only in circumstances where you regard the relationship with the supplier as less important to you than price advantage.

reducing process costs

electronic ordering

Electronic catalogues make it possible to simplify requisitioning, ordering and receipting processes and to accelerate the delivery process. The person makes the requisition via their computer; the order is transmitted electronically to the supplier within, say, five minutes; the goods are delivered the next day. Security checks are necessary, and good purchasing practice demands that the items 'on the list' fall within the control of a framework agreement, but electronic ordering is fundamentally simple. The main benefits are:

- less paperwork
- staff cuts – or the ability to free personnel for more strategic duties
- lower stock levels
- accurate capture of spend data
- unit price reductions

Electronic catalogues are ideal for low-risk, low-cost items such as stationery and consumables.

web portals and e-tendering

The time and cost of copying, packaging and despatching information to suppliers can be eliminated by the use of web portals. Suppliers can download buyers' enquiries from the portal in the form of, say, a Word document or Excel spreadsheet.

E-tendering allows suppliers to place their quotes and bids within a pass-worded area of a website. It further reduces processing costs and simplifies the system for evaluating bids: 'like for like' comparisons are much easier to make. As with electronic ordering, the clerical function is reduced. Other benefits include:

- accurate capture of tender data
- a shorter tender period

E-tendering can be used where supply market competition is required on important goods and services.

self-billing

Suppliers of high-volume goods and services no longer need to put invoices in the post. Buyers can agree to pay them 'x' days after receipt using electronic self-billing systems.

Electronic self-billing makes procedural and economic sense. From the purchase order or schedule, an organisation knows what it has ordered, from the receipt it knows what it has received. Provided the goods or services were up to scratch, it is contractually obliged to pay for them. Why bother receiving and processing an invoice?

One London Borough Council shed 16 people from its accounts payable team by adopting self-billing and by paying via electronically received consolidated invoices. Both the selling and purchasing organisations save on people and paperwork. There are other benefits that include better relationships between purchasers and suppliers.

Use self-billing to work with your closest, strategic suppliers and with those who supply you in high volumes. Do not, though, forget to keep a record of the VAT you have been charged.

eliminating risk

The supply chain is business-critical. Missing or weak links obviously threaten survival. When problems occur, internet search engines can be powerful tools to identify new sources of supply.

The internet creates a more competitive, more open market. It means that purchasers are less at the mercy of monopolistic suppliers who inflate prices or choose to restrict their offerings to bigger, more favoured customers.

Do not be constrained by any one supplier. Use e-sourcing to try to fight back. You just might be able to get unit prices down and shorten lead times.

promoting innovation

The right communications infrastructure will make it possible to link creative thinkers – whether in design, engineering, marketing or service provision – with their opposite numbers in key suppliers (and even key customers). This creates a mechanism for encouraging innovation and for refining new ideas. Drawings, plans, sketches and ideas can be transmitted and sent back within minutes, cutting design time and, ultimately, time to market.

There are risks attached to sharing information and granting access, but these are minimised in the context of a close, trusting relationship between purchaser and supplier. Provided intellectual property rights issues are addressed early on, there is no reason why this kind of ideas-sharing should not work to mutual benefit. Managed properly, it will greatly enhance strategic alliances with suppliers.

improving customer service

Information and communications technologies can greatly improve customer service, making it possible to track orders and to provide information quickly and efficiently. The sales team no longer has to say "We'll have to ring you back" if a customer calls with an enquiry: the details are there at their fingertips.

And customers are increasingly 'doing it for themselves', using their own computer screens to access the information they need, identify what they want, check delivery times and place their orders.

Online orders are processed by the organisation's own systems which, where necessary, 'communicate' with suppliers.

reducing lead times and inventory levels

E-procurement offers the opportunity of cutting both lead times and inventory levels. Ultimately, therefore, it can:

- [ ] increase customer satisfaction
- [ ] improve cashflow management – less money will be tied up in the warehouse or stockroom

Through systems integration, requirements can be transmitted and placed directly into the systems of their key suppliers. Add to this the ability to integrate with customers in the same way and days start to 'fall off' delivery schedules.

Because delivery is quicker, fewer items have to be held in stock.

Inventory can be cut back still further by matching order requirements to levels of available goods. If you know that your supplier has what you need – because you have looked into their system and seen the level of stock they hold – there is no great need to fill your warehouse.

If your systems are linked, it might be appropriate for your suppliers to manage your stocks for you, thus further cutting processing and human resources costs. The option of consignment stock (where payment is based on issue rather than receipt) can complement the benefits of 'e', further reducing the amount of capital tied up in stocks.

CASE STUDY: J N BENTLEY

Smaller private companies are often accused of shunning innovation and modern business practices, and of not investing in the IT systems to support them. It is not a charge that could be made against J N Bentley, a family-owned construction firm based in Skipton, North Yorkshire

Over the past three years, this civil engineering and building contractor has doubled its annual turnover from £17m to £34m. According to Martin Bentley, who leads the procurement team, the use of new technologies to interact with suppliers and customers has been a major factor in winning competitive advantage.

Since July 2001, all of the firm's 105 employees have had access to an internet-enabled contract management system that allows them to identify suitable products and suppliers and to place orders electronically. For busy site managers, this has made the purchasing process faster, cutting down on paperwork and allowing more time to supervise work.

Back at head office, the benefits include a clearer view of expenditure, shorter lead times, and administrative cost savings of more than £150,000 a year.

Innovation also seems to have helped J N Bentley to retain skilled construction workers in a tight labour market. Staff turnover since 2000 has fallen 1.7 per cent.

Crucially, the bespoke system allows customers to log in and see the actual costs being incurred on the projects they have commissioned. In an industry legendary for disputes over spiralling costs, such transparency is an important means of building trust.

CASE STUDY: J N BENTLEY

"Construction has always been very adversarial," says Bentley, "but in recent years there has been a move towards partnering in the supply chain and to the use of open-book trading. As a company, we wanted to take a step forward and embrace these initiatives. We also saw a situation where large national contractors were winning more business; as a smaller regional player, we needed to be able to compete with them."

Bentley's approach has attracted new clients, including Procter & Gamble and Cadbury Trebor Bassett, and strengthened relationships with valuable and long-standing customers such as Yorkshire Water. Meanwhile, partners such as concrete supplier Hanson Aggregates say the system has improved the clarity and accuracy of orders and helped ensure that invoices are paid on time.

Geraint John

Your stock levels should, ideally, reflect demand as well as availability. Under e-procurement, you can look also into the systems of your customers and then set stock levels according to their demand forecasts.

To see the potential of systems integration and e-procurement ask yourself the following questions:

- how much money is tied up in stock?
- how long would current stock levels last?
- what is the average lead time of key components?
- if we could reduce lead time by 10 per cent how much would we save?
- if 25 per cent of our stockholding could be managed by the supplier on a consignment stock basis, with self billing, how much would we save?

implementing an e-solution

Switching to e-procurement and e-sourcing might involve significant capital investment. How can you make sure you get a good return? There are several imperatives:

- be clear about the business case and realistic about the benefits
- choose ICT suppliers carefully

☐ make sure the technologies are deployed for strategic – as well as low-value, tactical – purchases

Once ICT is embedded in purchasing processes and playing a full part in purchasing activities, the strategy will be to apply human resources to maximise the advantages of the new environment. Attention will focus on those high-value, high-risk purchases that matter most. The management of supplier and customer relationships, of negotiating and of strategic sourcing will move up the agenda.

Freed from clerical, processing tasks employees will be able to deliver even more in terms of cost benefits, innovation and customer service.

conclusion

E-procurement and e-sourcing are tools to gain competitive advantage; they are not, however, solutions in themselves. Ultimately, they are only as good as the people and organisations who use them.

Properly managed, they can underpin the different strategies used by purchasing teams to meet business objectives and deliver real business benefits.

building a case for outsourcing

Steve Mullins, joint managing director, and Simon Steele, consultant, of PMMS Consulting Group, look at the issues that should inform outsourcing decisions

In 1996, the Institute of Management defined outsourcing as "the transfer of responsibility for one of an organisation's internal processes or activities to a third party, under a contract with agreed standards, costs and conditions".

Although still accurate, this simple description does not tell the whole story. Outsourcing has grown as much in complexity as it has in popularity. The 'transfer of responsibility' for functions such as IT and customer call-handling has raised questions about business control and about risk management (see chapter 10).

Meanwhile, high failure rates – research suggests that between 40 per cent and 80 per cent of contracts do not meet clients' business objectives – have given new impetus to the whole 'outsourcing versus in-house' debate.

EXECUTIVE SUMMARY

- [ ] clients must actively manage outsourcing projects

- [ ] a function should only be outsourced if there are clear business reasons to do so

- [ ] clear understanding of internal operations, of strategic goals and of customer needs is vital

- [ ] clients must make a thorough assessment of the specific outsourcing-related risks

The question of how deals are made and how contracts are managed has become pivotal.

This chapter looks at the best way to approach the procurement of outsourcing services. It focuses on factors that should influence the 'do-it-yourself or buy' decision.

the problem

The failure of outsourcing contracts usually stems from a failure of interpretation. Too often, companies have misunderstood what outsourcing means; as chapter 10 suggests, they have read the word 'transfer' as the word 'abnegate'. They have effectively entrusted major parts of their operations to a single and often not well-known or understood supplier directed by a minimum of internal management resources. On many occasions, they have outsourced without a practical means of achieving recourse for failure – except, that is, for litigation.

the solution

Successful outsourcing of key functions depends in large part on the realisation that the deal must be managed. A contract with an outsourcing company should be seen in much the same way as a contract with, say, an advertising agency. It must be client-led and aligned with the objectives of the business.

building a business case

It follows that directors must be able to demonstrate clear business reasons for outsourcing. They must take a rigorous, methodical approach to the outsourcing decision, addressing the following issues:

- [ ] the rationale for outsourcing – why do we want to do this?

- [ ] the options – what can and should be outsourced from the organisation's complex array of activities, functions and business processes?

- [ ] management commitment – do we have the level of support to ensure the programme can be delivered?

- [ ] competency – do we have the appropriate skill sets to manage the delivery of an outsourcing project?

- [ ] risk assessment – what are the risks associated with the outsourcing deal; and how will we manage them?

- [ ] supply-market competency – is the market sufficiently capable or mature enough to deliver the requirement?

☐ costs – how does the expense of running the function in-house compare with the expense of contracting out?

Some of these issues are discussed in more detail below.

the rationale

The rationale for transferring responsibility must be clear and logical. Too many companies outsource for the wrong reasons. They choose to hire a third party because of:

☐ corporate fashion – everyone else is doing it, so we might as well

☐ high-pressure lobbying/sales talk from major outsourcing companies or existing suppliers

☐ the desire to get rid of a function that is in a mess – a high-risk strategy that fails to address underlying weaknesses in internal systems

The focus should be on the potential business benefits of contracting out. Principal among these are:

☐ lower costs – the contractor has the leverage to negotiate better deals from suppliers; economies of scale are passed on to you

☐ increased efficiency – internal resources are redirected; managers get more time for strategic work

☐ improved cashflow – the transfer of assets to the supplier releases capital into your business

☐ improved performance – the specialist has the experience and the skills to do the job better

☐ competitive edge – the supplier uses its 'inside knowledge' of the market or sector to your advantage

☐ access to skilled staff – particularly relevant, perhaps, in the field of IT procurement

☐ access to scarce resources and/or technology

The client should identify the benefits that are most important to the business; these will then form the outsourcing rationale.

the options

The number of activities that can be outsourced has grown dramatically over the past 20 or so years. Outsourcing contracts range from the traditional – catering, cleaning, security and training – and more leading-edge areas – tactical procurement, reception duties, purchase transactions, and finance and tax – to radical options such as telesales, customer care, research and development, and the complete HR process. These categories are only a guide, but outsourcing is developing rapidly and today's radical will be tomorrow's leading edge.

So, how do you choose which functions to keep in-house and which to hand over? Key to the decision will be clear identification of core and non-core activities. The former category will probably include those operational elements that create or protect brand value, that are the business. (A national newspaper, for example, is very unlikely to outsource responsibility for the whole of its content.) The latter category, more secondary activities such as facilities management.

Computer giant IBM, which has used outsourcing services since the early 1990s, has been careful to retain internal control of those activities that:

- ☐ provide management and direction
- ☐ maintain competence and control
- ☐ differentiate it from its competitors
- ☐ sustain its USP

Core-competency analysis is not a simple task and requires much thought. 'Core' will not necessarily be the same thing as business-critical. Vital functions such as IT can be outsourced with no threat to organisational or brand integrity.

By the same token, some non-core activities may benefit from being left in-house; your customers, for example, might resent having to ring that remote, third-party call centre. Knowing your customers and their expectations will help to make your decision easier.

risk assessment

The risks associated with outsourcing vary almost as much as the potential benefits.

In identifying possible dangers and in devising mitigation strategies, companies will need to answer the questions below and on the next few pages.

How well do we understand the outsourcing marketplace for our requirement?

- ☐ is it national, European or global?
- ☐ who are the serious players?
- ☐ how well do we understand their managements, visions and strategies?
- ☐ what are their pricing policies?
- ☐ who are (and will be) the winners and losers?
- ☐ what are the key players' track records for related contracts?

How well do we understand our current operation?

- ☐ is it under-performing – and, if so, by what criteria/measurements?
- ☐ is it in a mess – and if so, why?

How 'digestible' is our requirement?

- ☐ what is the shape and size of the operation to be outsourced?
- ☐ can the existing market handle it?
- ☐ do similar projects account for a big or small proportion of suppliers' businesses?

How stable is our requirement?

- ☐ will volumes remain constant?
- ☐ what happens in the event of business downturn or of diversification into new areas?
- ☐ what happens in the event of acquisitions, mergers, de-mergers and divestments?

What is the risk that things will go wrong either during the transitional phase or post implementation?

- [ ] what's the service provider's track record in managing major change programmes?
- [ ] what is ours?

How experienced and skilled are we at managing supplier relationships?

- [ ] are we averse or inclined to close, partnership-style relationships?
- [ ] is our history one of arms-length, adversarial relationships?

Will we be able to manage suppliers?

- [ ] does their track record indicate any past 'manageability' problems?
- [ ] do we possess the skills/resources to manage them effectively?

Will we be able to change provider later?

- [ ] what does the contract say?
- [ ] did we contract with the current service provider in a way that negatively affected the rest of the market?
- [ ] are the logistics of our operations so closely linked that change would be impossible/highly costly/disruptive?
- [ ] how will the current supplier perform/behave during the exit transition?

Is there a risk that we'll be exploited?

- [ ] what are other customers' experiences?
- [ ] what form has customer exploitation taken?

What are the 'human' dimensions?

- [ ] are our two cultures aligned?
- [ ] how and when should we communicate our outsourcing decision to staff?
- [ ] is there a risk of plummeting morale during the transition?
- [ ] what will the effect of our decision be on the rest of the organisation?

- ☐ what, if any, are the implications under the Transfer of Undertaking (Protection of Employment) Regulations?

- ☐ are there any other legal or moral obligations to the existing staff?

- ☐ will a major redeployment/redundancy programme follow; if so, are we prepared for it?

- ☐ if the supplier is taking over our staff, what are its intentions?

supply-market competency

Outsourcing markets vary in maturity and in number and type of suppliers. The client must research the market thoroughly and ask whether the same supplier will be able to meet its requirements in all the countries it operates in. It must accept that it might not be feasible to 'globalise' the outsourcing decision. In some regions, such as Asia, markets for outsourcing differ widely in terms of both maturity and of the capability of suppliers. This will affect the outsourcing rationale – and, of course, the risk analysis.

Different supply markets demand inherently different approaches. In some mature markets, a tough, leverage-based approach might be right; in others, collaboration and partnership.

costs

Cost comparison is vital – without it, no meaningful business case can be constructed. Nonetheless, it is a tricky thing to get right. It depends on full identification of the client's own costs – including indirect costs and overheads – and a clear and accurate understanding of where a supplier's cost advantage might come from.

The issue is discussed in detail in the next chapter.

conclusion

Outsourcing contracts must be actively managed. Decisions must be informed by knowledge of the business and its customers and of the supply market.

Xchanging

*Xchanging Cost for
Service and Savings*

Radical Improvement of Non-core Activities

**For further Information
please contact**
Mary Norris
Xchanging Procurement Services

Telephone: 07831 411728
email: mnorris@xchanging.com

www.xchanging.com

delivering an outsourcing project

Steve Mullins of PMMS, and David Oates, sales and marketing director at Xchanging Procurement Services, offer a step-by-step guide to getting a good outsourcing deal

The previous chapter looked at how an organisation should evaluate the potential for outsourcing and seek to build a strong and objective case for purchasing outsourcing services. This chapter addresses some of the practical issues associated with managing an outsourcing project through to delivery: it looks at outsourcing from the proof-of-concept stage.

pre-contract steps

assessing the service

The scope of the service that is to be outsourced should be precisely and accurately defined; the client should have a clear idea of how it dovetails with parts of the business that will be 'left behind'.

The work done by your supplier should neither duplicate nor conflict with that done internally; you should outsource with due regard for the interdependency of 'remote' and internal functions.

> ### EXECUTIVE SUMMARY
>
> ☐ service level agreements must be consistent with your business objectives
>
> ☐ continually compare the performance of your suppliers with that of their peers
>
> ☐ make the terms of the contract clear, precise and comprehensive – get expert advice
>
> ☐ include clauses that protect intellectual property
>
> ☐ ensure suppliers place equal focus on service, process and cost reduction

Always remember that an outsourced function is not 'cut loose' from the business but still a part of it – and a part that affects the whole.

Where related services are being outsourced to different suppliers the issue also becomes one of managing the 'fit' between the respective contractors.

It might not be possible – or desirable – to outsource all the elements of what might be seen as a single service to a single company. In some markets, broad 'holistic' service players dominate; in others, niche companies and narrow specialists.

deciding on service requirements

The question of what level and standard of service the contract should stipulate is sometimes difficult to answer. This is especially true for those companies that have not taken a systematic approach to measuring performance. If you do not know whether a function has done well or badly (and on what criteria) how can you say what you want for it in the future?

The general rule is always to make sure that service levels are aligned with your business objectives. A design consultancy, for example, might want more out of facilities management contracts than, say, a haulage company.

Additionally, establish a governance body to manage and review service on at least a monthly basis.

contracting strategy

planning ahead

One of the golden rules for drawing up a contract is to think of future as well as current needs. As well as service requirements, key considerations include:

- the type of relationship and commercial arrangement sought
- market change
- business change
- aggregation and convergence of requirements
- technological developments
- demand patterns

PERFORMANCE MANAGEMENT

In a perfect world, the supplier would do all that he was contracted to without any prompting from the customer. In the real world, the need for some form of intervention is almost inevitable.

The client has two choices:

- [ ] wait until the service deteriorates and then fly into recovery mode
- [ ] set up an agreed, adequately resourced, process to measure all core aspects of service by means of key performance indicators (KPIs) – with the specifics identified and managed through a Service Review Board (SRB).

If it is agreed that the latter approach is better, then a further set of issues can be focused on:

What are the key measurement parameters?

- [ ] are they the ones used to measure the current operation?
- [ ] what is the market's view on measurement parameters?
- [ ] what measures do the suppliers' present customers use?
- [ ] what measures are needed to ensure the business case is realised?

Are there targets for improvement?

- [ ] does the agreement envisage or demand that performance improves over time?
- [ ] is continuous improvement part of the plan and part of the contract?
- [ ] what targets will be set; what process and resources will be used to monitor them?

How do we use service credits and debits?

- [ ] are they intended for performance both over and under target?
- [ ] what exact mechanisms are required to determine them?
- [ ] what arrangements are required for their payment?

retaining flexibility

Clients should ensure that the transition at the expiry of the contract is as smooth as at commencement. The office equipment company Xerox, for example, has its outsource contractors design their plans for insourcing – just in case.

Allied to this concept is the need to ensure that the performance of the outsourced service is systematically tracked.

retaining critical core competencies

Do not agree to the transfer of the commercial, technical and operational competencies you will need to direct and manage the provider. Keep at least some key personnel in-house.

retaining market awareness

Make it known in all negotiations that you wish to retain 'market awareness'. If you are to measure the performance of your supplier you will need to know how its competitors are doing. A respectable service provider who values your business will contractually agree to make its own benchmarking studies and share the results with you.

Openness is key to building that vital good relationship (see chapter 9) – and avoids the often disruptive and counter-productive process of asking the supplier to prove itself in another bidding war.

retaining competition

Set early performance targets to encourage competitive behaviour. Do not wait until contract expiry date to line up possible contenders: you want as short a delay as possible between termination and transfer.

the contract

the right agreement

The service of an experienced and effective outsourcing lawyer is essential in drawing up the contract. So too, however, is the input of the client: there might be specific commercial implications that only you can see.

style

The style of the contract will reflect the nature of the relationship. Questions to ask include:

☐ how mature is the current relationship with the probable outsource provider(s)?

- [ ] can we phase the implementation process?

- [ ] what type of relationship will we realistically begin with?

- [ ] what objectives have we set for the relationship?

- [ ] what is the level of trust between the parties?

- [ ] what have we learned from others about the service provider's approach to relationship management?

The nature of the relationship will, in turn, reflect the type of function being outsourced. You may not, for example, need to forge very close links with the cleaning contractor, unless you are a scientific research company, of course.

complexity

The level of contract complexity will be determined by:

- [ ] the nature of the service

- [ ] the number and scale of risks involved

- [ ] pricing issues and associated schedules

- [ ] the degree of flexibility needed to anticipate major technical or strategic change

core content

The contract must specify:

- [ ] precise service definitions

- [ ] service limitations – eg. hours worked; range of duties

- [ ] term, including notice period

- [ ] the personal relationships and lines of communication needed for the contract to work

- [ ] joint and several benchmarking responsibilities

- [ ] performance monitoring, measuring and review arrangements through formal review board

- ☐ conflict-resolution mechanisms

- ☐ change control procedures covering all eventualities

- ☐ asset transfer arrangements: who will own the assets at the contract end; what are the provisions for possible transfer or repurchase?

- ☐ the client's right to re-negotiate terms in changing business circumstances

- ☐ the right of the client or client representatives to carry out periodic 'audits' of the contract

payment structure

Ask whether:

- ☐ the contract enables the customer to share in productivity gains made by the provider

- ☐ the focus is on total cost reduction over time or on unit cost reduction

protecting intellectual property rights

The client must campaign vigorously for the protection of IPR and take the necessary steps to ensure that sensitive information is not passed on to its competitors. Terms and conditions could prevent the supplier working for specified competitors for a defined period of time.

locking in the project leaders

Name in the contract the people you see as being critical to the success of the project and insist that they work on your account for an agreed period.

Insert a 'non-poaching' clause to avoid the defection of your key people to the outsourcing company.

conclusion

The business case for outsourcing will fail without the right written agreement between client and contractor. Insist on clarity and precision from the outset.

MAKING A MEANINGFUL COST COMPARISON

How can a business determine in advance whether or not a contract will be cost-effective?

These are the key areas to look at:

current costs

☐ what is the total cost of ownership?

☐ have we done any coherent cost analysis?

☐ have we got a clear idea of the true impact of outsourcing on direct, variable, semi-variable and fixed overheads?

☐ what about the impact of outsourcing on our fixed-variable cost dynamics?

☐ if we outsource, will we simply re-deploy existing staff and assets and increase the total cost base?

☐ if we outsource part of the operation, what will the cost implications be for what remains?

If we un-source, do we have the resource and skills available today?

the suppliers' prices and costs

☐ did our tender/bid documentation and subsequent negotiations ensure pricing clarity?

☐ have we done any PPCA (cost modelling) on providers' proposed service-delivery processes?

☐ what are their margin expectations at the total and individual services levels?

☐ given their margin requirements, how do we feel about their ability to offer real cost advantages to us?

☐ what's their record on price stability?

☐ do they have a history of achieving substantial productivity gains but not sharing the benefits?

☐ do they have a history of driving income through contract variations?

☐ what might drive cost variability?

☐ what assumptions are we making about their pricing and cost structure and have we fully tested them?

☐ how dependent is their price on information they have gleaned from us and assumptions they have made – eg. overtime actuals?

MAKING A MEANINGFUL COST COMPARISON

☐ have Transfer of Undertakings (Protection of Employment) considerations been properly factored into their pricing?

economies of scale

☐ what are the providers' economies of scale?

☐ will they be passed on to us?

VAT

☐ is our VAT position a material issue here and, if so, has it been properly factored in to the cost comparison?

how to outsource procurement

David Oates, sales and marketing director at Xchanging Procurement Services, looks at the factors that make or break procurement outsourcing projects

As the opening chapter made clear, procurement is a strategic function. Any move to outsource any of it therefore demands careful direction.

This chapter deals with the key management steps involved in transferring some of the responsibility for purchasing to a third party. Much of the information it gives could equally apply to the outsourcing of other strategic functions; it can be read as a general guide to best practice.

establishing support within your organisation

Lack of sponsorship from within the organisation can doom an outsourcing project to failure. Outsourcing as a concept is often viewed by the procurement department as a synonym for redundancy. This naturally leads to a defensive attitude and, often, a will to see the project fail: turkeys do not vote for Christmas.

The problem can only be avoided by systematic top-down communication: the board should make clear its support for the outsourcing initiative, explaining why the decision has been taken, how and when the project will be implemented and what it will mean for those individuals involved in the procurement process.

EXECUTIVE SUMMARY

- ☐ the board must make known its commitment to the initiative and clearly explain the rationale

- ☐ consultation exercises must start early and continue for the duration of the contract

- ☐ project management and service review boards must be set up as forms of 'due diligence'

- ☐ the relationship between client and supplier must be an equal partnership

In real terms, the procurement department is rarely, if ever, completely outsourced. Indeed, the projects that have been most successful are those where only non-core or indirect procurement is outsourced. This means that, rather than losing their jobs, procurement professionals are able to work more effectively on core activities that are strategically important to the business. This positive shift in the role of the procurement professional must be communicated at every level of the organisation.

continuing consultation

The process of communication must start as early as possible – delays will allow rumours to circulate and ill-feeling to fester – and last for as long as the outsourcing project.

Ongoing consultation will help not only to secure permanent stakeholder 'buy -in' but also to identify and resolve problems.

One of the best ways of ensuring that all stakeholders are actively involved throughout the lifecycle of the project is to set up management and service review boards, staffed by representatives from both the client company and the supplier.

setting up management and service review boards

The role of the management board is to oversee the project and ensure its successful delivery. The role of the service review board is to ensure the continuing fulfilment of service commitments. In other words, the former manages the project; the latter, the client-supplier relationship. This separation helps limit the scope for conflict of interest: the management board can concentrate on the delivery of the commercial benefits of the project.

Both boards should be comprised of equal numbers of client and contractor staff. This approach helps to underline the principle that the 'moral ownership' of the project is jointly bestowed. It also means that the boards' position is more likely to be one of neutrality: the progress of the project and the quality of the service can be reviewed objectively.

The responsibility and accountability of each board should be formally and clearly defined.

identifying and replacing flawed processes

Before the outsourcing relationship can begin in earnest, it is necessary to identify and improve poorly defined and badly integrated procurement processes. What is being outsourced will ultimately only be as good as those functions it interrelates with. (See previous chapter.) Without the commitment to replace or 'repair' flawed processes, even the world's finest procurement team will be unable to deliver any real value.

A good, reputable outsourcing company will focus heavily on the state of relevant client operations, with significant efforts being put into service and process definition before the project starts its transaction phase.

taking a partnership approach

As has already been suggested, the relationship must be one of equal halves. Any attempt by the client to abdicate responsibility for the outsourced function or functions will be tantamount to business suicide.

The temptation to 'wash hands' will be strongest among those managers who fail to perceive procurement as a strategic function and to recognise that its various parts must form a coherent whole.

Companies that understand the importance of procurement and that have made a clear business case for outsourcing make the best clients. They will recognise that the contractor cannot, and should not, work in a vacuum. Although credible providers of business process outsourcing (BPO) will have extremely skilled and experienced practitioners with in-depth knowledge of a number of categories of spend, they will never be so reckless as to claim they know as much about a client's business as the client itself. They will rely on the company to disseminate information and share its expertise.

Continued dialogue will ensure that the supplier understands not only the client's business but also its culture. Without appreciation of corporate values, of ways of doing things, the outsourcing company cannot hope to integrate successfully.

Both parties must be committed to achieving effective communication across all stakeholders.

sharing the value

The best BPO providers are the ones that go that 'extra mile', that meet more than contractual obligations. They have the foresight to realise that rolling contracts depend on efforts to exceed client expectations. They therefore operate on the principle of gain-share, delivering as much value through financial savings as possible and then sharing that value with the client.

conclusion

Procurement outsourcing will be doomed from inception if:

- ☐ the board does not 'buy-in' to the deal
- ☐ the relevant stakeholders are ignored
- ☐ the outsourcing rationale and the implementation process are poorly defined
- ☐ there is no formal management or review structure
- ☐ flawed processes are not identified and put right
- ☐ the client abdicates responsibility
- ☐ the client fails to see procurement as a business-critical function

Outsourcing is a strategic decision that must be boardroom-led. When looking for the ideal client there is usually one thing at the front of a provider's mind: "a CEO with an agenda for change".

tales from the frontline

BAE SYSTEMS has chosen to use outsourcing to control part of its indirect procurement spend. David Oates, sales and marketing director at Xchanging Procurement Services, looks at what its experiences can teach us

In 2001, estimated global business-to-business procurement spend was $18tn. Of this, the majority was indirect spend, ie. procurement spend on things that don't become part of their outputs, but help to run the organisation.

That huge sums of money go on everyday things such as office supplies, furniture, travel services, car fleets and contract labour is one of the hidden facts of corporate life.

Media stories usually focus on core purchases. They tell us about powerful purchasing managers winning great pipe and well-head equipment deals for petroleum giants, or steel and sub-assembly deals for defence contractors. They tell us how competitors increase their buying power for key components through consortia such as Covisint, the buyer-controlled auction market for General Motors, Ford, Nissan, Renault and DaimlerChrysler.

Not many of them tell us that:

☐ indirect procurement accounts for 60 per cent to 80 per cent of all purchasing transactions

EXECUTIVE SUMMARY

☐ cutting indirect spend can make dramatic improvements to profit margins

☐ outsourcing to a single supplier can standardise and rationalise the procurement process

☐ ill-feeling between the provider and inhouse staff will derail the project

☐ when things go wrong, both parties must work together to find mutually acceptable solutions

☐ manufacturing, distribution, retail, financial and professional companies spend, on average, 40 per cent of their total revenue on indirect goods

Facts and figures like these make it clear that cutting indirect procurement costs could significantly improve profit margins. The question becomes: how can a company corral its indirect spend to achieve better results?

One of the answers is to outsource. Indirect spend is often fragmented across decentralised units and made by miscellaneous, disparate agents housed in back office functions such as human resources or general admin. Handing over responsibility to a single company creates, among other things, the potential for significant, cost-effective rationalisation.

This chapter looks at how BAE SYSTEMS has used outsourcing to manage part of its indirect spend of £800m a year. It aims to show the pitfalls – as well as the opportunities – of procurement outsourcing.

the background

In January 1999, a merger was proposed between British Aerospace and GEC's Marconi Electronic Systems to create a global aerospace and defence company. The new company, BAE SYSTEMS, employs more than 100,000 people and had a turnover of £13bn in 2001. It serves as a prime contractor and systems integrator for customers throughout the world, focusing on air, land, sea, space, and command and control market sectors.

Investors were promised that the synergies resulting from the merger would save more than £275m within three years of the deal being completed. While BAE SYSTEMS would continue to invest in its core capabilities in military aircraft, weapon systems, nuclear submarines and large commercial aircraft, all support functions were mandated to deliver significant cost savings.

controlling human resources spend

In human resources management, the set goal was to achieve a 40 per cent saving on an estimated £25m while maintaining the same level of service. BAE

SYSTEMS evaluated the options and decided that the best solution was to centralise, standardise and downsize HR operations – which employed 700 staff in 70 locations. Its chosen route to rationalisation was a 50/50 joint enterprise partnership with Xchanging, called Xchanging HR Services. The deal, signed in February 2001, was worth £25m a year.

The client subsequently transferred its HR assets and 500 personnel to the partnership, which delivers HR services via a web-enabled portal. Under the arrangement, BAE SYSTEMS gets guaranteed savings of 15 per cent – plus a share in any future profits as Xchanging attracts new clients to the venture.

As well as taking on BAE SYSTEMS' HR activities, Xchanging discovered a significant amount of related indirect spend managed within the HR functions for such items as health care, company cars, non-technical contract labour, training, and recruiting. It became very evident to the parties that this spend of approximately £80m per year actually dwarfed core HR spend.

The question became: how could BAE SYSTEMS improve the management of the huge volume of indirect spend that had previously been handled by its decentralised HR people? It was clear that the following capabilities were needed:

- [ ] category expertise: people who were experts at understanding and negotiating specific indirect spend categories such as car fleets and office supplies

- [ ] the right sourcing methods and tools: techniques and technologies to define, benchmark, research, analyse, negotiate, and manage indirect spend

- [ ] purchasing power: the ability to leverage better deals from suppliers by consolidating indirect spend within the company – or, better yet, across companies

- [ ] supplier appeal: the ability to attract excellent suppliers, not only by the promise of bigger contracts but also by the ability to reduce a contractor's transaction costs through efficient processes and prompt payment

- [ ] governance: the ability to govern indirect spend and to reap financial benefits

options for transforming indirect spend

Like all large organisations, BAE SYSTEMS had a number of viable options for getting these transformative capabilities:

- [ ] do it themselves
- [ ] hire a consultant
- [ ] join a consortium exchange
- [ ] outsource to an e-procurement company
- [ ] create an enterprise partnership

Because its indirect spend was integrated with the Xchanging HR Services deal, BAE SYSTEMS chose the last option, creating another jointly-owned enterprise partnership with Xchanging Procurement Services, in November of 2001, together with a ten-year supply deal that was initially worth around £80m a year.

Xchanging Procurement Services manages the entire supply chain for BAE SYSTEMS and its UK subsidiaries in specified indirect spend categories. Xchanging has exclusive procurement rights in these categories.

As a result, BAE SYSTEMS is obligated to purchase the category items through Xchanging Procurement Services for the duration of the contract, subject to Xchanging continuing to perform.

The contract initially covered seven categories of indirect spend:

- [ ] fleets
- [ ] non-technical contract labour
- [ ] learning and development
- [ ] healthcare
- [ ] permanent recruitment
- [ ] remuneration and benefits
- [ ] stationery

In order for buying to be transferred to Xchanging Procurement Services, the baseline spend had to be measured and approved and legal contracts had to be reviewed.

Xchanging Procurement Services estimated that the initial benchmarking and approval activities would take two months. Once the spend was transferred, the partnership would then apply the competencies needed for transformation.

teething troubles

Xchanging Procurement Services's forecasts were sadly over-optimistic. At times it took six months to transfer a category of spend to the partnership. Two factors caused major delays:

- [ ] the partnership had to liaise with and gain approval from a great number of BAE SYSTEMS managers
- [ ] spend verification led to adjustment of in-scope categories

liaison and co-ordination

To transfer a category of spend, Xchanging Procurement Services had to visit up to 30 BAE SYSTEMS sites, converse with up to 50 people in order to gain approval of the baseline.

Learning and development was a particularly difficult area to benchmark because the spend was highly decentralised and spread around more than 1,000 suppliers. Just gathering the right data was a Herculean task: the benchmarking exercise took almost six months.

In such a huge organisation communication of the process and approach to the task of baselining, to every corner of the company, was a real challenge. Equally, it did not necessarily sit high on the wider communities priority list. As with many change programmes, a degree of resistance to change had to be overcome, thereby slowing the pace.

Xchanging Procurement Services was under pressure to speed things up: under the terms of the agreement, it would not earn a profit until the baselines were approved. It became increasingly aggressive in seeking co-operation, which led to increased friction.

To resolve the problems, BAE SYSTEMS devoted more resources to managing the relationship between the two parties.

verification of spend

The contract called for approximately £80m in spend to be transferred to Xchanging Procurement Services in seven categories. By the middle of 2002, however, only £30m was with the partnership.

The figure for learning and development (£25m) had, for example, been over-estimated by 30 per cent. The shortfall seriously threatened Xchanging Procurement Services' ability to meet projected profitability targets.

Executives from both sides held many strategic planning sessions to try to close the gap. The partners agreed that it was in their joint interests for more than the intended critical mass of spend to be transferred. This would be achieved by adding eight more categories of spend, bringing the Xchanging Procurement Services-controlled spend to nearly £100m by year end 2002. The new categories included:

☐ travel (approx. £40m)

☐ printing (£3m)

☐ office furniture (£2m)

☐ computer consumables (£1.3m)

Despite the fact that the partnership's transaction and administration costs have increased – procuring 15 categories is clearly more expensive – it has reduced benchmarking cycle times significantly on categories by between 5-45 per cent, depending on the category.

conclusion

One of the most critical trust-building factors is operational delivery. As Xchanging Procurement Services continues to deliver the cost savings and improved service levels, the trust levels of the parties increased. Further evidence of the trust is demonstrated by BAE SYSTEMS plans to transfer more indirect spend categories to the partnership.

The experience of BAE SYSTEMS and Xchanging shows that:

- the ability to communicate the meaning of the partnership to all budget holders and users in the organisation is a vital component of the plan

- the outsourcer must be ready, and the customer must be willing, to help the partner traverse the political and bureaucratic terrain of its organisation

- the supplier must appreciate that aggressive approaches often backfire

- both parties must be willing to adapt to discoveries during due diligence

- the customer and the supplier must set realistic deadlines and targets

- the customer and supplier must align their objectives, but accept that there is no such thing as an instant partnership; that trust evolves over time

getting the right relationships

The key to working well with suppliers is remembering that one size does not fit all, says Brian Court, director and senior consultant with PMMS Consulting Group

As an organisation develops its supply market, the question 'what sort of relationship should we have with our suppliers?' inevitably arises. The traditional relationship, still common today, is mostly arm's length and adversarial.

The underlying assumption is that purchasing is a competition, where the purchaser outmanoeuvres the supplier in order to get the best deal. The purchaser shops around, asking sellers to compete on price, and bases decisions mainly on short-term considerations.

new ways of working

In the past 12 years, many purchasers have concluded that this is not the best way to do business and have been seeking out new ways of working. There has been a desire to move away from combative relationships to those involving greater co-operation between purchaser and seller.

The idea of close, long-term relationships, which has its origins in Japanese industry, has come to be known in the west as 'partnership sourcing'.

EXECUTIVE SUMMARY

- ☐ low-value contracts demand little interaction between buyer and seller
- ☐ partnership approaches are appropriate only where there is the potential to win competitive advantage
- ☐ effective partnerships depend on trust, transparency and the willingness to share risks
- ☐ long-term arrangements might conflict with the interests of lenders and shareholders

THE FULL-SERVICE STATIONERY CONTRACT

Specialist stationery suppliers now offer a full service. Rather than just fulfilling the stationery order, the best now monitor stock levels at point of use, replenish where necessary and provide a consolidated but detailed invoice regularly

They take on many of the activities that have previously been the responsibility of the purchasing organisation. The benefits for the purchaser are:

- ☐ less stock holding
- ☐ lower prices
- ☐ lower administration costs
- ☐ more time for strategic activities

the case for co-operation

The advocates of collaboration, and there are many, start from the premise that arm's length and adversarial relationships are wasteful and prevent both parties achieving the best results. Conversely, they say, companies that work together in a more co-operative manner enjoy reduced costs and other benefits.

There are many examples to support the argument. Take the case of the North American chemicals company that saved nearly $20m. The company, a major producer, needed to increase capacity. A key part of its new plant was a compressor train. It was predicted that the new compressor would cost $45m and be on the critical time path for the project. However, instead of inviting competitive bids, the chemicals producer decided to work co-operatively with one pre-selected compressor manufacturer. As a result, the compressor was removed from the critical path and the cost was reduced to $26m.

Some attempts at co-operation, however, have not been so successful. Resources have been wasted; results poor.

the portfolio approach

So what is the best way to work? The quick answer is that there is no one best way of purchasers and suppliers doing business. The most productive relationship will be dictated by the purchasing company, the supplier, the market and, especially, the nature of the transaction. An effective purchasing organisation will almost certainly have a variety of supplier relationships within its overall portfolio.

the spectrum of relationships

It is possible to define a spectrum of purchaser/supplier relationships. This is illustrated in the box below.

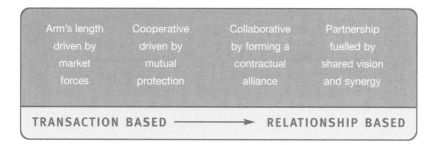

| Arm's length driven by market forces | Cooperative driven by mutual protection | Collaborative by forming a contractual alliance | Partnership fuelled by shared vision and synergy |

TRANSACTION BASED ——————➤ RELATIONSHIP BASED

The relationships between the two parties become closer and of longer duration as we move from the left to the right of the spectrum.

At the extreme left, there will be little contact or interaction. The relationship will consist of an agreement to purchase goods and supplies, almost certainly on a one-off basis. The purchaser will solicit bids from several suppliers and select the best proposition. The relationship will be very arm's length and there will be no intention to extend it beyond the immediacy of the contract. Here, the purchaser depends on a competitive market to deliver a reasonable deal.

As we move to the right, the relationship becomes closer and may last for longer. Under the 'co-operative' category, we might expect purchaser and seller to agree on the supply of goods or services over a period of time and under agreed conditions, thus creating some efficiencies and cost savings. Here, the supplier might undertake certain additional duties that it can perform more economically than the purchaser. (See box on stationery contracts.)

The relationship becomes even closer under 'collaborative' agreements, whereby the supplier works with the purchaser to improve cost, design and service in return for a longer term contract.

EXAMPLES OF EFFECTIVE PARTNERSHIPS

☐ A province in China decided to install a new telecommunications system. It was seeking a low-cost system but, more importantly, one that would not take long to become operational. It invited seven telecommunications providers to submit bids.

The company that won the contract had formed an exclusive strategic partnership with a switch provider. Well before the invitation to bid, both companies had worked together to take cost out of the system and to find ways of setting it up more quickly.

This gave them the competitive edge required to win the business and reap the rewards. The telecommunications company won business it might not otherwise have got; the switch manufacturer made an additional sale.

☐ A manufacturer of aero engines worked with a turbo blade manufacturer on a new design. The blade manufacturer received no payment for development, but was richly rewarded when an engine sale was made.

The ultimate relationship is a 'partnership' or 'strategic alliance'. In this scenario, purchaser and seller create a situation where the success of each is linked to the other. Together, they seek out ways of driving out cost from the entire supply chain or of creating some other competitive advantage.

This type of relationship is not easy to achieve but has the potential to improve performance.

choosing the type of relationship

How, then, do purchasers decide which type of relationship will best suit their particular needs? The decision will depend on many factors, including

☐ the value and significance of the spend – if the spend is low and/or has little strategic significance, then the relationship is more likely to be towards the left-hand side of the spectrum

☐ the frequency of spend – if expenditure on a particular category is infrequent there will be no justification for anything other than an arm's length relationship

☐ competition in the supply market – if the market is crowded, a competitive rather than a collaborative approach will probably get the best results. If there is a reduced number of suppliers or a technical or price breakthrough is being sought, a closer relationship will probably be more productive

☐ potential – where there is scope for considerable long-term benefits, the relationship will move towards the right-hand side

☐ attitude and track record of supplier – suppliers with excellent track records and a pro-active approach might be good candidates for closer liaison and eventual partnership

defining a partnership

Partnerships have specific characteristics. What distinguishes them from other business relationships?

A purchaser/supplier partnership can only exist if:

☐ purchaser and seller in some way share risk and reward

☐ there is a climate of openness and trust

☐ there is scope for joint activity that creates added value

If any of these three factors, described in further detail below, is absent, the partnership will be bogus.

risk and reward

Purchaser and supplier must work closely together to improve product offerings and create new opportunities. Both parties must be prepared to invest time and effort with no certainty of reward. Their fortunes will become linked together, they will share both the risks of failure and the rewards of success. See box, 'Examples of effective partnerships'.

openness and trust

There can be no true partnership without transparency – and no transparency without confidence in the other party.

To move forward, each party must reveal competitively-sensitive information on costs, research, market plans, etc. There must be a high level of what Mari Sako, professor of management studies at Templeton College, Oxford, has defined as 'goodwill trust'. This can be characterised as an open commitment or a willingness to do more than is formally required. It means being prepared to accede to a request from the partner or to react to any observed opportunity that would improve performance.

It is implicit in the partnership arrangement that the parties refrain from opportunistic behaviour and from exploiting the other's weaknesses, and that there is no use of coercive power.

joint activity to create added value

If the two parties cannot work together to create additional value, the partnership is meaningless. If there is no additional value there is a danger that the relationship will degenerate into a competition for the share of the existing value. It is only when the cake can be made larger that the focus moves from share to size.

partnership risks

Partnership sourcing has its detractors. In particular, there are doubts about whether Japanese-style partnership practices can be successfully transported to the West. The long-term nature of partnership deals is somewhat at odds with the Western need to satisfy banks and the stock market by producing good short-term profits. Suppliers, in particular, look to large, short-term margins to sustain profitability and hence share price.

In Japan, in contrast, the institutions have tended to work more closely with industry, setting goals that have had a horizon of 10 years or more.

There is already a body of evidence that suggests that 'partnership' type relationships are proving hard to sustain outside of Japan – and, more recently, inside Japan itself as recession takes its toll.

This is not to say that partnerships cannot be developed profitably – but rather to emphasise the need that they need skilful handling.

managing partnership risks

Purchasers must select their partners carefully. Often, the transition to true partnership will depend on significant cultural and attitudinal change, on the ability to reverse perhaps long-held traditions. Inflexibility is something that will rule a supplier out as a potential partner. So, too, is lack of commitment from the top. Beware of any company that seems to pay only lip service to the partnership ideal – or to be at the mercy of internal or external forces that might inhibit good results.

Partnership sourcing will only work when both parties feel that they are not being exploited. They must have the security of knowing that the relationship is on a sound footing and that it will continue for the foreseeable future. Both parties must be able to discuss problems frankly and constructively, realising that a disagreement does not signify the end of a relationship, but the beginning of its improvement.

It is difficult for parties with no previous history of a relationship to come together as successful partners. A partnership arrangement is the culmination of progressively closer relationships – of a continual build up of trust and commitment.

Competitive bidding is an unlikely starting point for a partnership. Adversarial in nature, it does not provide the kind of information that is vital when selecting a partner. You need to be able to see the potential partner as they really are – not as a player in a game.

conclusion

Relationships between purchasers and sellers necessarily vary in nature. A partnership should only be the preferred choice where there is true potential to gain competitive advantage. And, they should only be undertaken after very careful evaluation of all of the alternatives.

In the West, the purchaser/supplier relationship has traditionally been an adversarial one. The mere expression of good intentions will not be sufficient to change it. Purchasers should, therefore, be highly selective in their approach to partnerships, putting their trust only in those who deserve it.

managing
supply-side risks

Ken James, chief executive of The
Chartered Institute of Purchasing & Supply,
looks at ways of reducing supply chain risks
to corporate success and reputation

In recent years, the management of risk has moved up the corporate agenda. The 1999 Turnbull report on corporate governance made it clear that a company's systems of 'internal control' should cover not only major financial risks but also risks arising from legal, health and safety, reputational and environmental issues.

EXECUTIVE SUMMARY

☐ directors have a duty to stake-holders to control purchase and supply management risks and manage reputation

☐ dependence on any one supplier is dangerous

☐ sourcing policies must reflect corporate social responsibilities

☐ professionally drafted contracts help to minimise risk exposure

The supply chain is often where the different kinds of risks converge. Loss of supply has serious commercial consequences; defective goods are threats to product safety and, therefore, legal liabilities; sourcing policies have clear implications for the environment and for society at large, and the potential to damage a company's image and reputation.

Effective purchasing and supply chain management is, then, at the heart of organisational risk control.

defining risk management

Risk management demands that directors ask, 'What if?'. But it is not the same thing as risk-aversion. It accepts risk as a fact of business life – and looks at how it can best be handled.

It consists of three distinct, but inter-related disciplines: risk analysis, risk assessment and risk mitigation.

risk analysis

This identifies all the things that might go wrong with a project or activity and looks at the probability of each happening.

Correctly undertaken, risk analysis is a vital component in effective management, allowing all risks to be recognised and objectively assessed.

The complexity of the analysis should reflect the complexity of the project. High-value, high-risk projects such as IT-systems procurement clearly require detailed work.

Usually, it is convenient to categorise technical risks and financial risks in terms of their likely probability. Risks that cannot be easily controlled or managed might need to be insured against. It is important, though, that the insurance policy does not come to be seen as a risk-management substitute. Insurance claims are undesirable – a risk in themselves. Staff need to be encouraged to take great care of high-value, business-critical goods and services – in much the same way as they need to be encouraged to take health and safety issues seriously.

risk assessment

Risk assessment calculates the probable impact of a risk on an organisation. It is therefore crucial in determining risk-avoidance and risk-mitigation strategies.

Preventative efforts will need to be directed towards the highest-impact 'events'. These are often those that are statistically least likely to occur. In particular, there will need to be disaster recovery plans in place in the event of terrorist attack, arson, flooding, etc.

risk mitigation

This is the actual anticipation of risk. It will involve contingency planning and the identification of those parties best able to manage the risks concerned. It will ensure that the right people have the right powers to mitigate risks.

purchasing and supply management risks

security of supply

A breakdown or interruption of key supplies can result in operational break-down (eg. halted production lines), increased costs and damage to a brand or a corporate reputation.

To manage the risk is, fundamentally, to manage supplier relationships. Detailed and thorough supplier appraisal procedures are advisable. Beware of suppliers with potentially serious financial problems: they are very likely to let you down.

In general, you should look for suppliers whose approach and ethos are broadly consistent with your own. A 'cultural fit' greatly improves the chances of effective communication – and, therefore, of minimal supply and demand problems. Working in partnership with you, your key or strategic suppliers will be able to alert/help you to anticipate potential risks within the supply chain.

Effective supplier relationships require a delicate balancing act. Ideally, you should be close to your suppliers without being dependent on them. Over-reliance on any one company significantly increases supply-side risks. Have contingency plans in the event of supplier failure – research the market (see chapter 5). Do not have all your eggs in one basket; try to spread the risk.

Organisations faced with the possibility of a dangerously high level of supplier dependency can be tempted to transfer the element of risk to the supplier. This, however, can be a risk in itself: the supplier may react by raising prices.

Risk transfer will only work if the third party has some degree of control over the eventuality. Some organisations make the mistake of offering incentives or rewards to suppliers to take on risks they can do nothing about.

quality

Quality control is a big part of risk control. If externally acquired inputs are not up to standard, an organisation's outputs will suffer. The results can, again, be operational breakdown, increased costs and damage to reputation/brand. Effective sourcing strategies will mitigate the risks.

information 'asymmetry'

When one party to a contract knows more than the other a dangerous power gap can arise.

There is a measurable degree of risk in dealing with suppliers who have more knowledge of the product than you do – and who make use of this knowledge to charge higher prices, for instance.

The purchasing organisation should try to eliminate this imbalance by being fully familiar with the product and its position in the marketplace; in this context, joint product development initiatives with the supplier can be seen as a risk-mitigation strategy.

outsourcing

Outsourcing non-core activities can bring significant operational benefits – not least reductions in costs, but it can also create further risks. The three main areas of risk are:

- loss of control
- loss of intellectual property
- damage to brand/reputation

The sportswear manufacturer Nike fell foul of outsourcing risk several years ago when it handed some of its manufacturing to overseas sweatshops. The damage to its good name was considerable.

To mitigate the risks involved in outsourcing, research potential contractors thoroughly. And make sure you stay close to the project or operation. Remember that outsourcing is a way of delegating responsibility – not abrogating it. Ultimately, you remain in charge.

regulation

Organisations must comply with the regulatory environment they operate in. Failure to do so can result in court action and be a serious reputational risk.

In recent years, regulations from both the UK and the EU have addressed issues such as the triple bottom line – a company's responsibilities to the environment and society as well as the economy – and corporate governance. A company is now, more than ever before, expected to act ethically. This raises important supply-side questions. Should a company use suppliers in the Third World who are dependent on child labour? Should it buy goods, services or capital items from companies that pollute the environment or waste the world's resources?

Whether you care about such issues or not, you cannot ignore their significance. They represent significant reputational and, therefore, commercial risks. Purchasing and supply management policy must reflect this reality.

contracts

The agreement made between organisation and supplier is of critical importance. Poorly and unprofessionally drafted, it will increase risks. Correctly and professionally drafted, it will be an effective risk-mitigation tool.

The contract should provide an early definition of the relationship between purchaser and seller, stipulating what is expected from both parties. If one of the agreed aims, for example, is to work together to reduce product costs, this should be clearly stated.

Crucially, the contract should give a precise indication of renewal dates and of notice periods. The purchaser should be able to terminate the agreement in a reasonable and fair timeframe.

For significant contracts, a business case should be made, detailing the reasons for the investment and the expected return. This is a kind of due diligence process – without it, the risk that money will be squandered greatly increases.

At the pre-contract stage, it is often useful to ask bidders to state in their tender documents which risks they would be willing to take responsibility for; these can then be the subject of negotiations during the bid clarification process.

risk from the suppliers' perspective

Remember that risk management is not the preserve of the purchasing organisation. If a supplier perceives a risk to be present (for example, uncertainty about their suppliers or doubts about any of their customers) then they will build in a safety margin. This will obviously have cost implications for their trading partners.

conclusion

Effective risk and reputation management should be embedded in the organisation's culture. It should be a clearly defined responsibility in day-to-day decision-making.

Regular monitoring will be necessary to ensure the mitigation methods remain effective.

RISK MANAGEMENT SPIN-OFFS

To spot a risk is, sometimes, to spot an opportunity. Effective risk management can highlight the need for a better way of doing things – and add value. Some of the potential benefits are:

- ☐ reduced waste of resources
- ☐ less need for fire-fighting
- ☐ better focus on aims and objectives
- ☐ greater stability – particularly valuable at times of market uncertainty or unpredictability
- ☐ improved relationships with suppliers and customers
- ☐ improved value for money, potentially leading to increased margins and/or market growth

CHECKLIST FOR THE CHIEF EXECUTIVE

1. do you know how much your organisation is spending externally?

2. if yes, do you know how much is spent on each category of spend and with which supplier? (A category is a range of purchases – eg. energy, IT.)

3. do you know the total cost of the purchases you make, rather than just their price? (Such costs will include: the costs of the procurement/payment processes; the whole 'lifecycle' costs of major purchases – eg. machines, buildings.)

4. do you know how much value your suppliers provide and create for your organisation's success and reputation?

5. do you know who your key suppliers are?

6. do you have pro-active, close relationships with your key suppliers?

7. do you understand the risks inherent in the purchases you make? Are you managing them effectively?

8. do you know what you should outsource and what you should not outsource?

9. are you outsourcing services successfully?

10. are you managing suppliers of outsourced services successfully?

11. do you know what your purchasing strategies are; are they aligned to your business strategies?

12. do you have appropriately skilled people developing and managing your purchasing strategies?

13. what proportion of your external spend is managed by your purchasing professionals?

14. if the answer to the last question is not 100 per cent, why not? And, what are you doing about it?

15. how do you support your purchasing people to ensure they achieve appropriate business benefits?

16. do you direct your purchasing people to limit their focus to reducing prices by x per cent each year or do you direct them to achieve cost-effective, risk-controlled added value?